Behind the Shadows of *Romeo*

A WILLIAM SHAKESPEARE BIOGRAPHY BOOK FOR KIDS

Children's Biography Books

BABY PROFESSOR

EDUCATION KIDS

Speedy Publishing LLC

40 E. Main St. #1156

Newark, DE 19711

www.speedypublishing.com

Copyright 2017

In this book, we're going to talk about the life and works of William Shakespeare. So, let's get right to it!

WHO WAS WILLIAM SHAKESPEARE?

William Shakespeare, also known as the "Bard of Avon," was an author as well as an actor. The word "bard" means poet. He wrote plays as well as poems and he is sometimes called the national poet of England. His works have been famous around the world for more than four centuries, but little is known about his personal life.

WILLIAM SHAKESPEARE

WILLIAM SHAKESPEARE

There are only a few court records to indicate the details of his life. Because of this, his identity is largely a mystery. Some historians don't feel positive that the plays attributed to him were really written by him.

WHEN AND WHERE WAS SHAKESPEARE BORN?

There are no birth records available for Shakespeare, but there is a record of his baptism at a church called Holy Trinity. The church was located in a market town by the name of Stratford-upon-Avon and his baptism took place on the 26th of April in the year 1564.

HOLY TRINITY CHURCH,
STRATFORD-UPON-AVON

Scholars believe he was born three days earlier on the 23rd, so it's been recognized as his official birthday.

The town where he was born was a country town in England with the Avon River running through it, situated about 100 miles west of the city of London.

SHAKESPEARE'S FAMILY

There are a few records that provide some details about Shakespeare's family life. His mother, Mary Arden, was an heiress who owned land. His father, John Shakespeare, was a successful merchant working with leather.

SHAKESPEARE'S FAMILY

SHAKESPEARE'S HOME AT NEW PLACE, STRATFORD-UPON-AVON

OCKWELLS, BERKSHIRE.

In addition to running his profitable business, John Shakespeare held official positions as alderman as well as bailiff. These positions were similar to a mayor's position today. William was a middle child with two older sisters and three younger brothers. Records show that the family's fortune decreased in the late 1570s.

SHAKESPEARE'S EDUCATION

Very little is known about William Shakespeare's education. Historians believe that he attended the King's New School located in Stratford. This school taught the basic skills of reading and writing as well as the classic works of literature.

YOUNGER WILLIAM

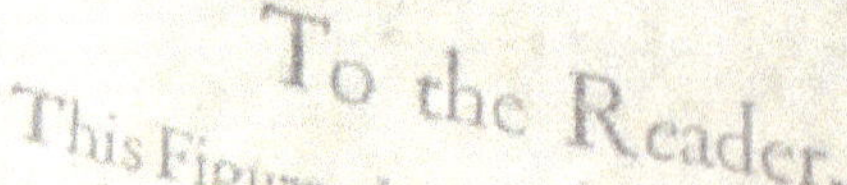
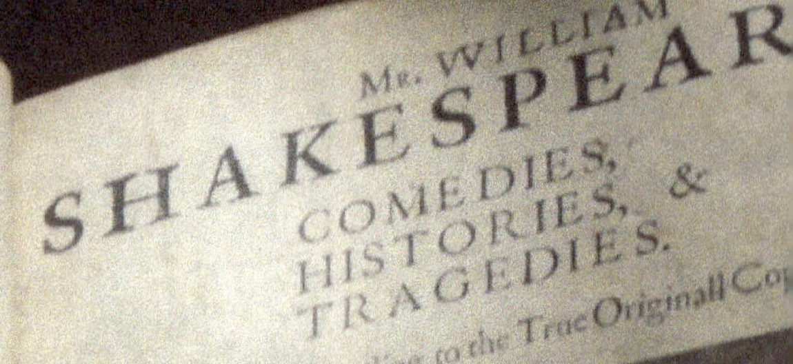

Mr. WILLIAM
SHAKESPEARE
COMEDIES,
HISTORIES, &
TRAGEDIES.

Published according to the True Originall Copies.

To the Reader.

This Figure, that thou here seest put,
It was for gentle Shakespeare cut;
Wherein the Grauer had a strife
with Nature, to out-doo the life:
O, could he but haue drawne his wit
As well in brasse, as he hath hit
His face; the Print would then surpasse
All, that vvas euer vvrit in brasse.
But, since he cannot, Reader, looke
Not on his Picture, but his Booke.

B. I.

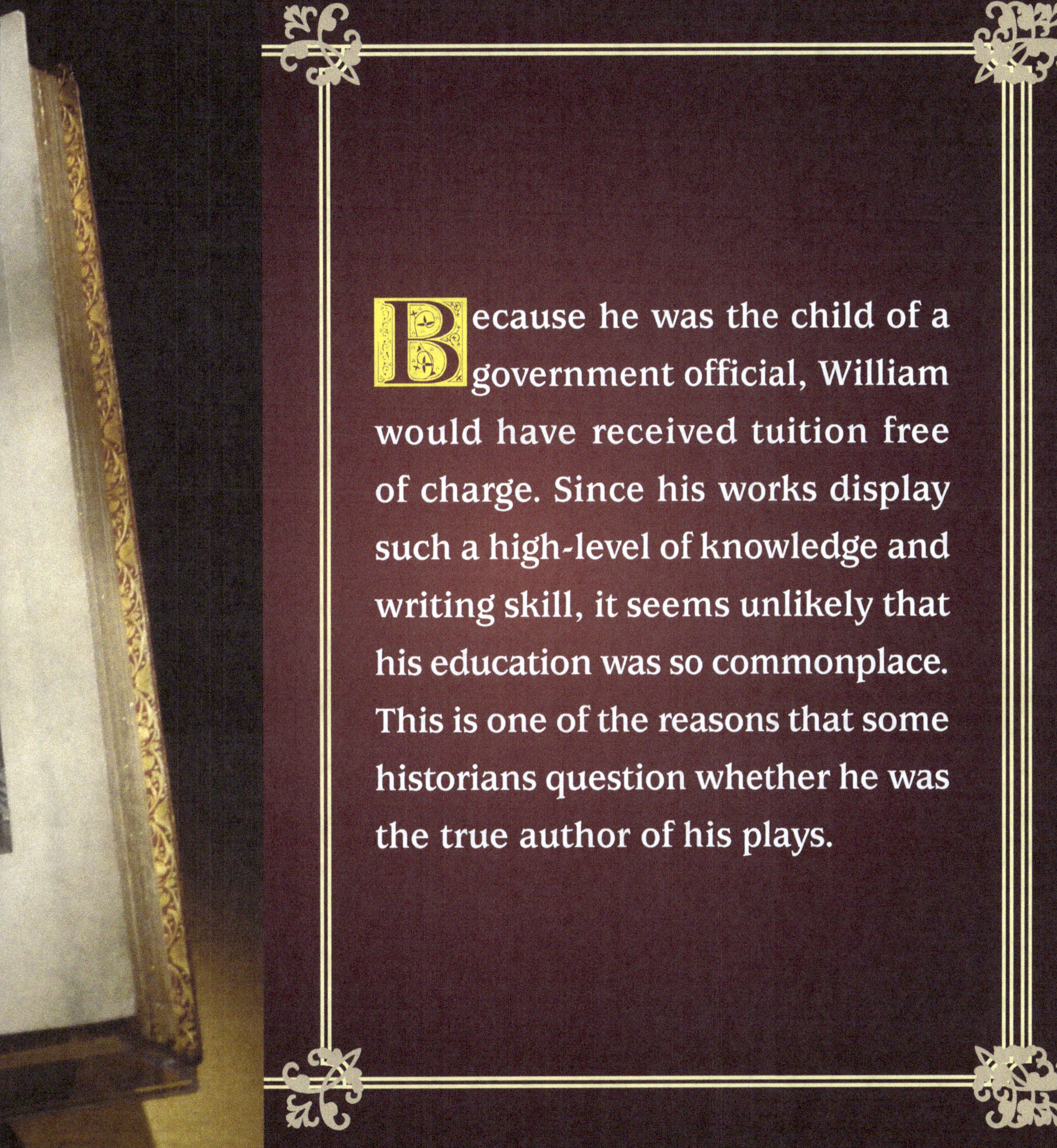

Because he was the child of a government official, William would have received tuition free of charge. Since his works display such a high-level of knowledge and writing skill, it seems unlikely that his education was so commonplace. This is one of the reasons that some historians question whether he was the true author of his plays.

MARRIAGE AND CHILDREN

William Shakespeare and Anne Hathaway were married in November of 1582 in the city of Worcester located in the province of Canterbury. William was only eighteen years of age when they married and Anne was eight years older than he was, which was unusual in those days.

ANNE HATHAWAY

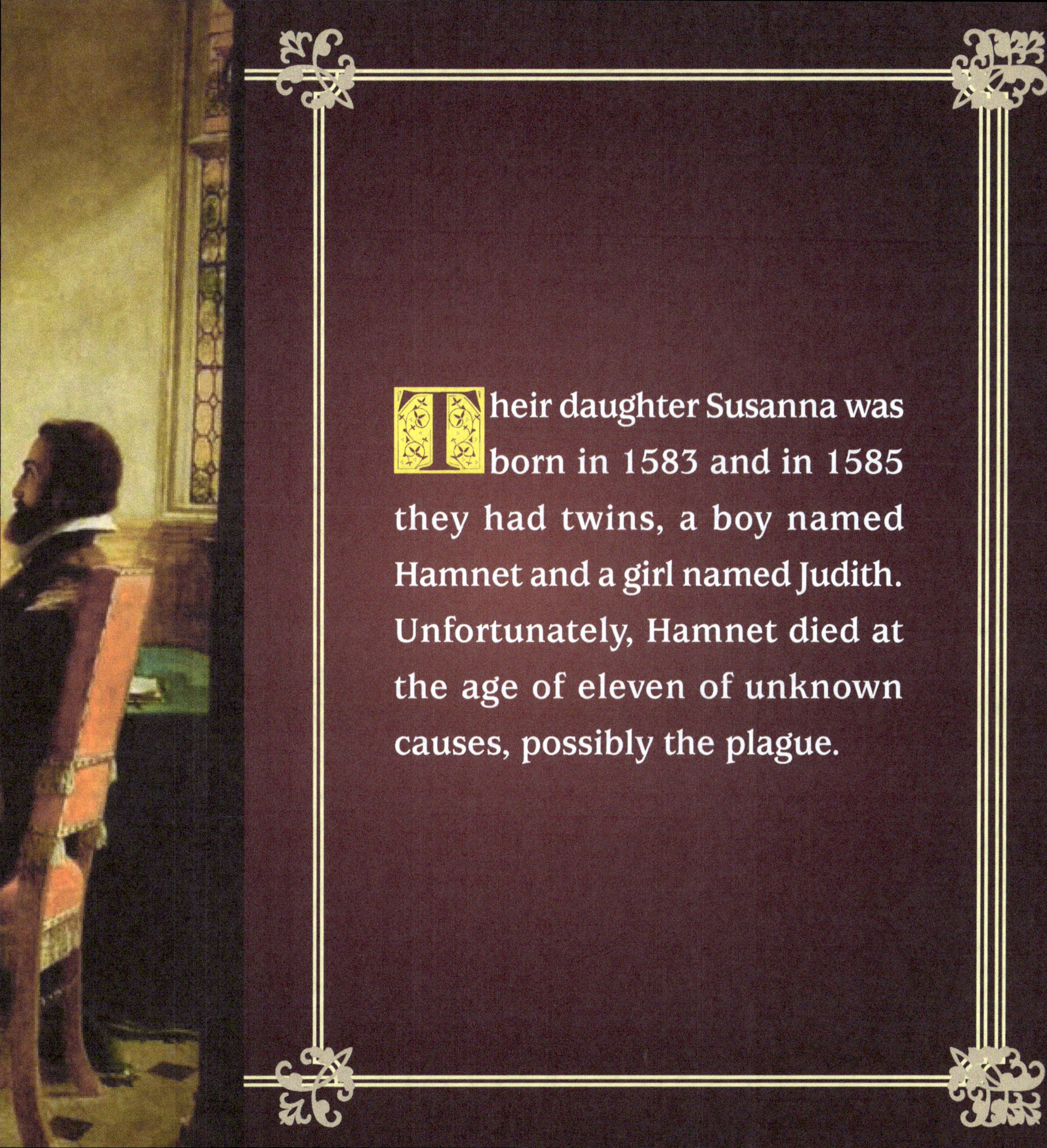

Their daughter Susanna was born in 1583 and in 1585 they had twins, a boy named Hamnet and a girl named Judith. Unfortunately, Hamnet died at the age of eleven of unknown causes, possibly the plague.

THE KING'S MEN

After the birth of his twins, there are no records of Shakespeare's life for seven years. No one knows exactly how he was earning a living during this time period.

By the start of the 1590s, there are records showing that he was a partner in an acting company in London.

LONDON, 16TH CENTURY

KING JAMES I

He was involved with this acting group both as an actor and playwright for most of his career. After King James I was crowned in England in 1603, the company changed its name from Lord Chamberlain's Men to the King's Men.

The actors in the company were well known and Shakespeare was selling his writing as popular literature by this time. The theater culture was not respected by the nobility, but the wealthy were patrons of the arts, so Shakespeare's work became known in these social circles.

SCENE FROM "KING JOHN"
AT DURY LANE THEATRE

WRIOTHESLEY SOUTHAMPTON

THE ACTOR AND PLAYWRIGHT

At the start of his career, Shakespeare attracted the attention of the Earl of Southhampton, Henry Wriothesley. He dedicated his first two published poems to the Earl. By the year 1597, Shakespeare had already written and published 15 of his total of 37 plays. His plays were highly successful and they still are today.

SHAKESPEARE'S HOUSE, STRATFORD

Because of his new wealth, he was able to buy a large house, which his family called New House. It was a long journey from Stratford to London, about four days travel by horse.

It's believed that Shakespeare lived and worked in London both writing and acting. He traveled home once a year during Lent because the theater was closed at that time.

SHAKESPEARE'S GLOBE THEATER

SHAKESPEARE'S GLOBE THEATER

Shakespeare and his business investors constructed their own theater in the year 1599. It was built on the southern bank of the Thames River and they named it the Globe. Six years later, he purchased real estate leases near Stratford.

his investment doubled in value and yielded a profit of 60 pounds every year. As well as a writer and actor, he was now an entrepreneur, and this regular income gave him more time to write his plays.

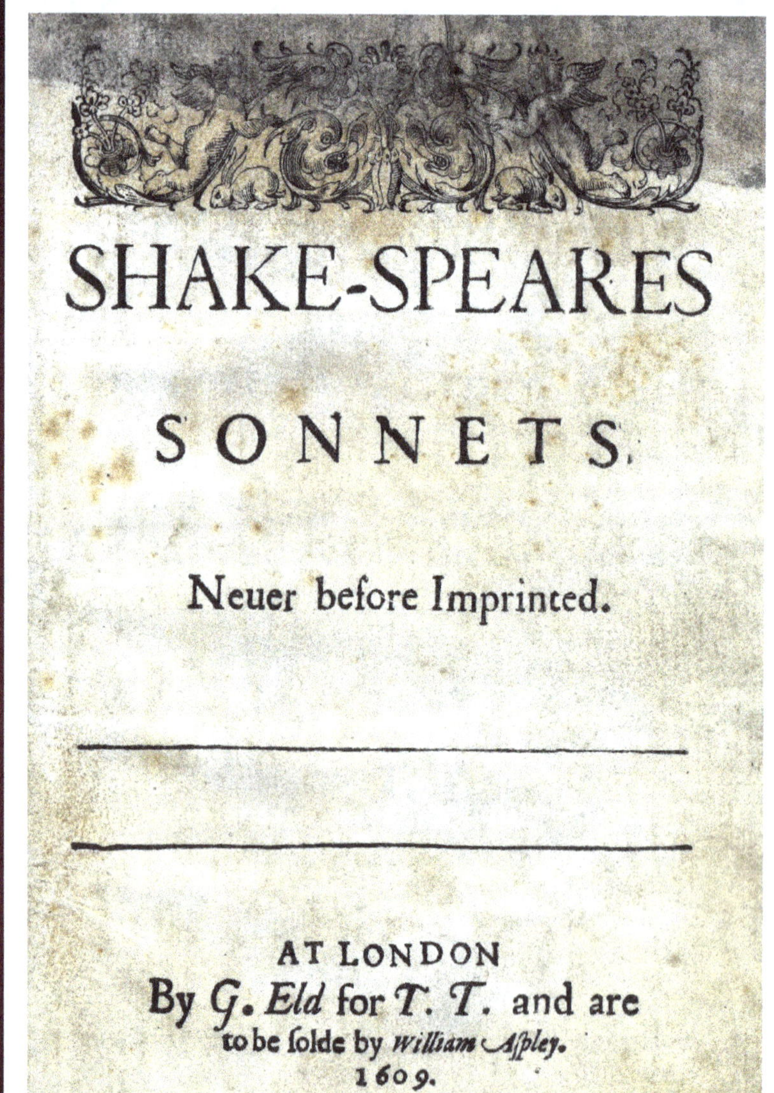

A PAGE FROM SHAKESPEARE'S SONNETS

SHAKESPEARE'S WRITING STYLE

As Shakespeare continued to write, his style changed over the years. At the beginning, his writing was filled with metaphors and phrasing that was formal and elaborate. Sometimes these words didn't line up well with the plot of the story or the characters. However, he quickly re-invented this style to suit his own ends, and created a stream of words that was more free and flowing.

e used a metric pattern known as iambic pentameter, which has five metrical feet. Each foot consists of a syllable that's unstressed followed by one that is stressed. He didn't write in rhyme. Within his work are passages that don't follow this rhythm and are either just simple prose or other forms of poetry.

During his lifetime, Shakespeare completed 37 plays and he collaborated on others as well. He also wrote 157 sonnets, a form of poetry.

SHAKESPEARES

SHAKESPEARE GRAVE
STRATFORD-UPON-AVON

SHAKESPEARE'S DEATH

Records show that Shakespeare was buried at Trinity Church on the 25th of April 1616, which means that he passed away when he was 52 years old. In his final will and testament, he left the bulk of his estate to Susanna, his daughter.

DID SHAKESPEARE WRITE HIS PLAYS?

The majority of scholars who study Shakespeare's work believe that he wrote his own plays. In addition to his name on the title pages of his published works, they also cite examples of authors and critics who wrote about him and his works.

SHAKESPEARE'S CRITIC

Edward Dere ... Earle of Oxford
Lord high Chamberlaine of En
Married 1st Ann Daughter to
Wm Cecil Lord Burghley
Eliz Daughter to Thos Tren
of Roucester in Com St
and died 24th of June 16

EDWARD DE VERE 1575

ther groups, such as the Shakespeare Oxford Society, have argued that the 17th Earl of Oxford, Edward de Vere, was the true author of the works. They show the similarities between his work and Shakespeare's.

They put forth the argument that Shakespeare didn't have the educational background to create the elegant prose and rich characters that live in the pages of his plays.

SHAKESPEARE'S MOST FAMOUS PLAYS

Here is a list of Shakespeare's most famous plays:

Romeo and Juliet, written in 1594, is about the tragic love story of two children from families who are enemies.

ROMEO AND JULIET

Midsummer Night's Dream, written in 1595, is a comedy about a group of fairies that try to solve the romantic troubles of mortals who are lost in the woods. It's a magical comedy.

The Merchant of Venice, written in 1596, is a comedy about a nobleman from Venice who doesn't pay a loan he owes to a Jewish merchant.

Much Ado About Nothing, written in 1598, is a comedy that combines hilarious humor with serious topics like honor and shame. In this story, a young couple that are soon to be married work to trick two people who don't get along to marry each other.

SINGING ROUND THE STAR ON TWELFTH NIGHT

Twelfth Night, written in 1599, is a comedy about identity and love that is lost.

Hamlet, written in 1600, is a tragedy about a young man who thinks about his own death while seeking revenge for his father.

Othello, written in 1604, is a drama about racism in 16th century Venice.

Macbeth, written in 1605, is a dark tragedy about a Lord from Scotland who commits a murder after being persuaded to do so by his wife.

King Lear, written in 1605, is about a tyrant who loses his mind in his old age.

The Tempest, written in 1611, is about a sorcerer who gets revenge on his enemies by using magic.

SUMMARY

For more than 400 years, William Shakespeare's plays have been performed throughout the world. He was a literary genius. Although his works are famous, little is known about his personal life.

There are only a few court records that provide an outline of the major events of his life. In fact, his background and experiences are so mysterious that some historians question whether he really wrote the plays that are attributed to him.

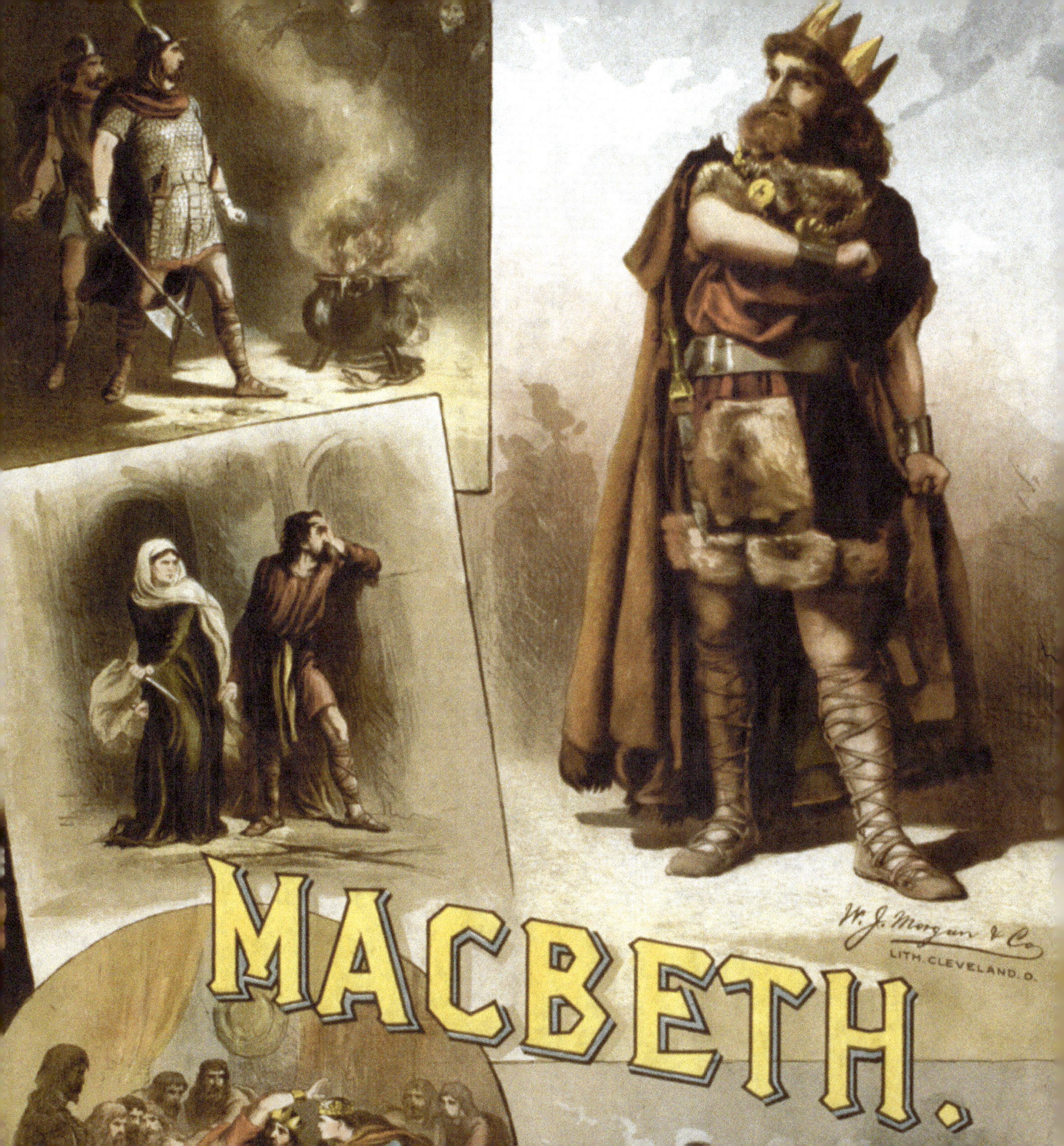

MACBETH.
W. J. Morgan & Co
LITH. CLEVELAND. O.

wesome! Now that you've learned about Shakespeare's life, you may want to read about other influential people who became famous during the Renaissance in the Baby Professor book Who Became Famous during the Renaissance? History Books for Kids.

Visit

www.BabyProfessorBooks.com
to download Free Baby Professor eBooks
and view our catalog of new and exciting
Children's Books